ŚRĪ MANAḤ-ŚIKṢĀ

Splendid Instructions to the Mind

ŚRĪ MANAḤ-ŚIKṢĀ

Splendid Instructions to the Mind

by Raghunātha Dāsa Gosvāmī

Volume One

Translated by Hari Pārṣada Dāsa

Illustrated by Jñānāñjana Dāsa

Illumination Education
Padma Inc.

Volume One
Version 1.2 (February 2017)

Published by Padma Inc., 2017
Hillsborough, NC, USA.

Printed by CreateSpace, an Amazon.com company.
Available from Amazon.com and other retail outlets.

Designed by Michael Best.
Set in Adobe Arno Pro.

DEDICATION

This edition of *Manaḥ-śikṣā* is dedicated to the pleasure of the residents of Vṛndāvana (*goṣṭhālayiṣu sujane*), as well as to those persons who aspire for their company.

CONTENTS

NOTES FOR THIS EDITION

The reader may wonder why a new edition of Raghunātha Dāsa's Gosvāmī's *Manaḥ-śikṣā* is needed. Over the years, many devotees of Kṛṣṇa expressed a longing for a trustworthy, literal translation of both the verses of *Manaḥ-śikṣā* and Bhaktivinoda Ṭhākura's commentary. We have tried our best to produce such a translation. Additionally, this edition contains Bhaktivinoda's song meditations on the original verses — the first time these songs are being published. This edition is also the first to be illustrated, a response to Raghunātha Dāsa Gosvāmī's use of metaphors and similes — tigress, ropes of wicked deeds, jewel of love, and so forth — that practically beg for paintings. Bhaktivinoda's commentary is also filled with descriptions which inspire illustrations.

The color illustrations are designed for deep meditation on each verse. In many cases, the details of those paintings are based on related descriptions from various *śāstras* and works of the *ācāryas*. The black-and-white drawings are based on the twelve verses as well as Bhaktivinoda's commentary, both prose and song.

We have produced this work as two printed volumes — one in color for meditation and the other in black-and-white for more in-depth study. The second volume adds significantly to our understanding of the original text by including the commentary of contemporary Vaiṣṇavas. We hope and trust that our expansion of the ocean of nectar in this way is pleasing to the predecessor *ācāryas*. *Manaḥ-śikṣā* was written as a guide for serious practitioners of *bhakti-yoga*, and it is helpful for such practitioners to have commentary which relates the eternal principles in this centuries-old work to current applications.

When reading the commentaries by Jayādvaita Swami, Śivarāma Swami, Śacīnandana Swami, and Bhaktivijnana Goswami, the reader should keep in mind that they were originally spoken seminars. Additionally, Bhaktivijnana Goswami's seminars were translated from Russian.

Readers familiar with BBT publications will likely notice that this edition uses lowercase for pronouns connected with the divine, as well as lowercase for descriptions of the divine that are not proper nouns (such as "divine couple"). Our reason is that Śrīla Prabhupāda wanted books to be in line with current scholarly standards. Such was his rationale for insisting on the use of diacritics rather than phonetic spellings for Sanskrit. Scholarly standards change with time and circumstance, and it is desirable, therefore, that our publications reflect current usage in order to follow Prabhupāda's desire.

Discerning readers will also note that the word-for-word translations of Raghunātha Dāsa Gosvāmī's verses follows the order of words in the translations rather than in the Sanskrit. We have adopted this method as both Bhaktivinoda Ṭhākura and his son, Bhaktisiddhānta Sarasvatī, favored it in their own publications. Because to a large extent this book is Bhaktivinoda's book, we felt it appropriate to follow his preference.

In Bhaktivinoda's commentary, there were six instances where we were able to use Śrīla Prabhupāda's translations for verses the Ṭhākura quoted. Those are noted in the text as being from the *Bhagavad-gītā*, *Śrīmad-Bhāgavatam*, or *Caitanya-caritāmṛta*.

Prints of the twelve color pictures and some of the black-and-white drawings are available at www.radharani.com.

The publishers

MANAḤ-ŚIKṢĀ AT A GLANCE

Verses 1-3: Qualification for the inner path of spontaneous attraction to Kṛṣṇa in Vṛndāvana

Verses 4-7: The process of eliminating obstacles, going subtler and closer to the root with each step by the mercy of, and love for, Kṛṣṇa and his devotees

Verses 8-11: Engaging in our eternal spiritual position through taking shelter, meditating, and serving Kṛṣṇa's internal, pleasure potency

Verse 12: Glories of these verses

MANAḤ-ŚIKṢĀ AT A GLANCE, EXPANDED

Verses 1-3: Qualification for the inner path of spontaneous attraction to Kṛṣṇa in Vṛndāvana

- Basic humility and lack of pride: a mentality conducive to face and eliminate one's inner contaminations, to serve others, and to beg for mercy
- Loving affection for everyone and anything connected with Kṛṣṇa in Vṛndāvana
- Detachment from materialistic activities on the path of karma
- Desire for loving service
- Engagement in chanting the Hare Kṛṣṇa mantra, Gāyatrī mantras, and worshiping Vraja Kṛṣṇa as taught by guru(s) in the path of Lord Caitanya through Svarūpa Dāmodara Gosvāmī and Rūpa Gosvāmī

Verses 4-7: The process of eliminating obstacles, going subtler and closer to the root with each step by the mercy of, and love for, Kṛṣṇa and his devotees

- Verse 4 — Problems: Absorption in mundane topics, desires for liberation, and desires for the opulences of Nārāyaṇa; Solution: Serve Rādhā and Kṛṣṇa in Vṛndāvana to receive a jewel of love of God.
- Verse 5 — Problem: Wicked deeds fueled by lust, anger, greed, and

so forth; Solution: Cry for help from the devotees of the killer of Baka (Deceit).

- Verse 6 – Problem: Deceit and pretense; Solution: Immersion in a bath of love for Rādhā and Kṛṣṇa (the artistic singer and the lifter of Govardhana Hill).
- Verse 7 – Problem: Desires for fame and honor; Solution: Service to a very exalted devotee of Kṛṣṇa.

Verses 8-11: Engaging in our eternal spiritual position through taking shelter, meditating, and serving Kṛṣṇa's internal, pleasure potency

- Kṛṣṇa, the lifter of Govardhana eliminates our wickedness, gives us glowing love of God to drink, and engages us in worshiping his *hlādinī-śakti*, Rādhā, the artistic singer.
- We drink and taste varieties of flavors of love of God by hearing about, mediating on, worshiping, and serving in various ways – Kṛṣṇa, Rādhā, Lalitā, Viśākhā, Rādhā-kuṇḍa, and Govardhana.

Verse 12: Glories of these verses

- Singing or trying to understand these verses gives one the jewel of service to Rādhā and Kṛṣṇa in Vṛndāvana as a follower of Śrī Rūpa Gosvāmī.

METER OF *MANAḤ-ŚIKṢĀ* FOR SINGING AND CHANTING

The meter for the verses of *Manaḥ-śikṣā* is *śikhariṇī*, the same meter that is used in the *Jagannāthāṣṭakam*. Each verse is divided into four *pādas*, which each consist of 17 syllables. The *pādas* are further divided into two parts of six and eleven syllables. The metrical scheme is as follows (⏑: a light syllable, –: a heavy syllable):

⏑ – – – – – | ⏑ ⏑ ⏑ ⏑ ⏑ – – ⏑ ⏑ ⏑ – |

VERSE ONE

गुरौ गोष्ठे गोष्ठालयिषु सुजने भूसुरगणे
स्वमन्त्रे श्रीनाम्नि व्रजनवयुवद्वन्द्वशरणे ।
सदा दम्भं हित्वा कुरु रतिमपूर्वामतितरां
अये स्वान्तर्भ्रातश्चटुभिरभियाचे धृतपदः ॥

gurau goṣṭhe goṣṭhālayiṣu sujane bhū-sura-gaṇe
sva-mantre śrī-nāmni vraja-nava-yuva-dvandva-śaraṇe
sadā dambhaṁ hitvā kuru ratim apūrvām atitarāṁ
aye svāntar bhrātaś caṭubhir abhiyāce dhṛta-padaḥ

aye—O; *bhrātaḥ*—brother; *svāntaḥ*—my inner self, my mind; *hitvā*—having given up; *dambham*—pride; *sadā*—always; *kuru*—please do; *apūrvām*—unprecedented; *atitarām*—excessive; *ratim*—attachment; *gurau*—to Śrī Guru; *goṣṭhe*—to the *goṣṭha* (the abode of cows), Vṛndāvana; *goṣṭha-ālayiṣu su-jane*—to the devotee residents of the *goṣṭha* Vṛndāvana; *bhū-sura-gaṇe*—to the earthly devotees (Vaiṣṇavas and *brāhmaṇas*); *sva-mantre*—to one's confidential mantra; *śrī-nāmni*—to *śrī-nāma,* the holy names of the Vṛndāvana couple; *vraja-nava-yuva-dvandva-śaraṇe*—in the shelter of the fresh youthful couple of Vraja, Śrī Śrī Rādhā-Kṛṣṇa; *dhṛta-padaḥ*—holding your feet; *abhiyāce*—I beg you; *caṭubhiḥ*—using pleasing words.

O dear brother! O mind! Having given up all pride, please develop unprecedented and excessive attachment to Śrī Guru; to Śrī Vṛndāvana, the abode of cows; to the devotee residents of Vṛndāvana; to all the devotees on this planet; to the confidential mantra [given by Śrī Guru]; to the holy names of Śrī Śrī Rādhā-Kṛṣṇa; and to the process of surrendering to the fresh youthful couple of Vraja. Holding your feet, I beseech you with sweet words.

Nandagrāma, as described in *Ānanda-vṛndāvana-campū* by Kavi-karṇapūra.

VERSE TWO

न धर्मं नाधर्मं श्रुतिगणनिरुक्तं किल कुरु
व्रजे राधाकृष्णप्रचुरपरिचर्यामिह तनु ।
शचीसूनुं नन्दीश्वरपतिसुतत्वे गुरुवरं
मुकुन्दप्रेष्ठत्वे स्मर परमजस्रं ननु मनः ॥

na dharmaṁ nādharmaṁ śruti-gaṇa-niruktaṁ kila kuru
vraje rādhā-kṛṣṇa-pracura-paricaryām iha tanu
śacī-sūnuṁ nandīśvara-pati-sutatve guru-varaṁ
mukunda-preṣṭhatve smara param ajasraṁ nanu manaḥ

nanu—indeed; *kila*—certainly; *na*—do not; *kuru*—do; *dharmam*—pious acts; *na-adharmam*—nor sinful acts; *śruti-gaṇa-niruktam*—which is spoken of in the Vedas and supporting literature; *iha*—here; *vraje*—[residing] in Vraja; *tanu*—please expand upon; *rādhā-kṛṣṇa-pracura-paricaryām*—the profuse service of Śrī Śrī Rādhā-Kṛṣṇa; *manaḥ*—O mind; *ajasram*—unceasingly; *smara*—remember; *śacī-sūnum*—the son of Śacī; *nandīśvara-pati-sutatve*—[as being] the son of Nanda Mahārāja; *guru-varam*—[and] Śrī Guru; *mukunda-preṣṭhatve*—[as being] one who is dear to the Lord; *param*—topmost.

Indeed, do not perform any pious acts prescribed in the Vedas and supporting literature, or sinful acts forbidden in them. Staying here in Vraja, please perform profuse service to Śrī Śrī Rādhā-Kṛṣṇa. O mind, unceasingly remember the son of Śacī as the son of Nanda Mahārāja, and Śrī Guru as the dearest servant of Lord Mukunda.

Serve Rādhā along with Kṛṣṇa, son of Nanda Mahārāja. Nanda Mahārāja gives young Kṛṣṇa to Rādhā who appears as a youthful forest goddess. Then Kṛṣṇa assumes his own youthful form and they wed. This *līlā* is described in the *Brahma-vaivarta Purāṇa* and Prabodhānanda Sarasvatī's commentary to *Gīta-govinda*.

VERSE THREE

यदीच्छेरावासं व्रजभुवि सरागं प्रतिजनुर्
युवद्वन्द्वं तच्चेत्परिचरितुमारादभिलषेः ।
स्वरूपं श्रीरूपं सगणमिह तस्याग्रजमपि
स्फुटं प्रेम्णा नित्यं स्मर नम तदा त्वं शृणु मनः ॥

yadīccher āvāsaṁ vraja-bhuvi sa-rāgaṁ pratijanur
yuva-dvandvaṁ tac cet paricaritum ārād abhilaṣeḥ
svarūpaṁ śrī-rūpaṁ sa-gaṇam iha tasyāgrajam api
sphuṭaṁ premṇā nityaṁ smara nama tadā tvaṁ śṛṇu manaḥ

śṛṇu—listen; *manaḥ*—O mind; *yadi*—if; *iccheḥ*—you desire; *āvāsam*—residence; *sa-rāgam*—with loving attachment; *vraja-bhuvi*—in the land of Vraja; *pratijanuḥ*—in every birth; *cet*—if [you desire]; *paricaritum*—to serve; *yuva-dvandvaṁ tat*—that youthful couple, Śrī Śrī Rādhā-Kṛṣṇa; *ārāt*—while staying nearby; *abhilaṣeḥ*—you desire; *tadā*—then; *tvam*—you; *nityam*—always; *sphuṭam*—clearly; *smara*—remember; *nama*—offer obeisances; *premṇā*—with love to; *svarūpam*—to Śrī Svarūpa; *śrī-rūpam*—to Śrī Rūpa; *sa-gaṇam iha*—with all associates staying here in Vṛndāvana; *tasya-agrajam api*—and also Śrī Rūpa's elder brother Śrī Sanātana.

Listen, O mind. If you desire, in every birth, to reside in the land of Vraja with loving attachment and to serve the youthful couple Śrī Śrī Rādhā-Kṛṣṇa in close proximity, then clearly remember and offer obeisances to Śrī Svarūpa, to Śrī Rūpa and his associates in Vṛndāvana, and to Śrī Rūpa's elder brother, Śrī Sanātana.

One should desire residence with loving attachment in the land of Vraja, attracted to a particular mood that is prominent among the *vrajavāsīs*. A practitioner then internally follows devotees such as Raktaka and Patraka in *dāsya-bhāva*, Subala, Śrīdāmā, and Ujjvala in *sakhya-bhāva*, Nanda, Yaśodā, and Rohiṇī in *vātsalya-bhāva*, or the *gopīs* headed by Śrī Rādhikā in *śṛṅgāra-rasa*.

VERSE FOUR

असद्वार्तावेश्या विसृज मतिसर्वस्वहरणीः
कथा मुक्तिव्याघ्रया न शृणु किल सर्वात्मगिलनीः ।
अपि त्यक्त्वा लक्ष्मीपतिरतिमितो व्योमनयनीं
व्रजे राधाकृष्णौ स्वरतिमणिदौ त्वं भज मनः ॥

asad-vārtā-veśyā visṛja mati-sarvasva-haraṇīḥ
kathā mukti-vyāghryā na śṛṇu kila sarvātma-gilanīḥ
api tyaktvā lakṣmī-pati-ratim ito vyoma-nayanīṁ
vraje rādhā-kṛṣṇau sva-rati-maṇi-dau tvaṁ bhaja manaḥ

manaḥ—O mind; *visṛja*—abandon; *asat-vārtā-veśyā*—the prostitute named mundane talk; *mati-sarvasva-haraṇīḥ*—the plunderer of all intelligence; *na śṛṇu kila*—do not listen at all to; *kathāḥ*—talks; *mukti-vyāghryāḥ*—the tigress named liberation; *sarva-ātma-gilanīḥ*—the devourer of all souls; *api tyaktvā*—also give up; *lakṣmī-pati-ratim*—attachment to the husband of Lakṣmī, Śrī Nārāyaṇa; *vyoma-nayanīm*—leading to Vaikuṇṭha; *itaḥ*—here; *vraje*—in Vraja; *tvam*—you; *bhaja*—serve; *rādhā-kṛṣṇau*—Śrī Śrī Rādha-Kṛṣṇa; *sva-rati-maṇi-dau*—the givers of the jewel of their own love.

O mind, abandon the prostitute of mundane talks, who plunders all intelligence. Do not listen at all to the stories of the tigress named *mukti* (liberation), who devours all souls. Moreover, also give up attachment to the husband of Lakṣmī, Śrī Nārāyaṇa, who only leads one to Vaikuṇṭha. Instead, here in Vraja, serve Śrī Śrī Rādha-Kṛṣṇa, who give one the jewel of their own love.

While in Vraja, serve Śrī Śrī Rādhā-Kṛṣṇa, the givers of the jewel of their own love. Rādha decorates Kṛṣṇa's hair and topknot with pearls in a jeweled pavilion. This *līlā* is described in *Govinda-līlāmṛta* 99-103.

VERSE FIVE

असच्चेष्टाकष्टप्रदविकटपाशालिभिरिह
प्रकामं कामादिप्रकटपथपातिव्यतिकरैः ।
गले बद्ध्वा हन्येऽहमिति बकभिद्वर्त्मपगणे
कुरु त्वं फुत्कारानवति स यथा त्वां मन इतः ॥

asac-ceṣṭā-kaṣṭa-prada-vikaṭa-pāśālibhir iha
prakāmaṁ kāmādi-prakaṭa-patha-pāti-vyatikaraiḥ
gale baddhvā hanye 'ham iti bakabhid-vartmapa-gaṇe
kuru tvaṁ phutkārān avati sa yathā tvāṁ mana itaḥ

iha—here [in this world]; *prakaṭa-patha-pāti*—attackers of the sparkling path [of devotion]; *vyatikaraiḥ*—the mob; *prakāmam*—by my own desire; *kāma-ādi*—[who are] lust, etc.; *gale baddhvā*—binding the neck; *vikaṭa-pāśālibhiḥ*—with dreadful nooses; *kaṣṭa-prada*—troublesome; *asat-ceṣṭā*—of wicked endeavors; *hanye aham iti*—I am being killed; *kuru tvam*—you cry out; *phutkārān*—pitieously; *iti baka-bhid-vartmapa-gaṇe*—like this to devotees of Kṛṣṇa, the killer of Baka; *manaḥ*—O mind; *avati sa yathā*—so that they will save; *tvām*—you; *itaḥ*—from these enemies.

"While here on the revealed path of devotion, I have been attacked by the gang of my own lust, etc., who have bound my neck with the troublesome dreadful ropes of wicked deeds. I am being killed!" Cry out piteously like this to the devotees of Śrī Kṛṣṇa, the destroyer of Baka. O mind, they will save you from these enemies.

To the saintly devotees of the Lord, headed by Nārada, Bhīṣma, and Arjuna, I offer my respectful obeisances. May they protect us on the shining path of *bhakti*.

VERSE SIX

अरे चेतः प्रोद्यत्कपटकुटिनाटीभरखर
क्षरन्मूत्रे स्नात्वा दहसि कथमात्मानमपि माम् ।
सदा त्वं गान्धर्वागिरिधरपदप्रेमविलसत्
सुधाम्भोधौ स्नात्वा त्वमपि नितरां मां च सुखय ॥

are cetaḥ prodyat-kapaṭa-kuṭināṭī-bhara-khara-
kṣaran-mūtre snātvā dahasi katham ātmānam api mām
sadā tvaṁ gāndharvā-giridhara-pada-prema-vilasat-
sudhāmbhodhau snātvā tvam api nitarāṁ māṁ ca sukhaya

are—O ruffian; *cetaḥ*—mind; *katham*—why; *dahasi*—do you burn; *ātmānam*—yourself; *api mām*—and me [the soul]; *snātvā*—by bathing; *kṣaran-mūtre*—in the trickling urine of; *bhara-khara*—the great donkey named; *prodyat-kapaṭa-kuṭināṭī*—full-blown hypocrisy and duplicity; *sadā tvam*—[instead] you should always; *snātvā*—by bathing; *nitarām*—always; *sudhā-ambhodhau*—in the nectarean ocean of; *gāndharvā-giridhara-pada-prema-vilasat*—the love emanating from the lotus feet of Śrī Śrī Gāndharvikā-Giridhārī; *sukhaya*—delight; *tvam*—yourself; *api māṁ ca*—and me too.

O ruffian mind! Why do you burn yourself and me [the soul] by bathing in the trickling urine of the great donkey of full-blown hypocrisy and duplicity? Instead, you should always bathe in the ocean of love emanating from the lotus feet of Śrī Śrī Gāndharvikā-Giridhārī, thereby delighting yourself and me.

One should bathe in the water of love emanating from the lotus feet of Śrī Gāndharvikā, the artistic singer, and Śrī Giridhārī, the lifter of Govardhana Hill.

VERSE SEVEN

प्रतिष्ठाशा धृष्टा श्वपचरमणी मे हृदि नटेत्
कथं साधुप्रेमा स्पृशति शुचिरेतन् ननु मनः ।
सदा त्वं सेवस्व प्रभुदयितसामन्तमतुलं
यथा तां निष्काश्य त्वरितमिह तं वेशयति सः ॥

pratiṣṭhāśā dhṛṣṭā śvapaca-ramaṇī me hṛdi naṭet
kathaṁ sādhu-premā spṛśati śucir etan nanu manaḥ
sadā tvaṁ sevasva prabhu-dayita-sāmantam atulaṁ
yathā tāṁ niṣkāśya tvaritam iha taṁ veśayati saḥ

dhṛṣṭā—unchaste; *śva-paca-ramaṇī*—dog-eating woman; *pratiṣṭhā-āśā*—desire for prestige; *naṭet*—dances; *me hṛdi*—in my heart; *katham*—how can; *śuciḥ*—pure; *sādhu-premā*—chaste lady of love for Kṛṣṇa*; *spṛśati*—touch; *etan*—this heart; *nanu manaḥ*—O mind; *sadā tvam*—you should always; *sevasva*—serve; *atulam*—incomparable; *prabhu-dayita-sāmantam*—beloved devotee commander of the Lord's army; *yathā*—so that; *saḥ*—he [the devotee commander]; *tāṁ niṣkāśya*—throw her [the prostitute] out; *tvaritam*—immediately; *taṁ veśayati*—establish her [*premā*]; *iha*—here [in the heart].

As long as the unchaste, dog-eating woman of desire for prestige dances in my heart, how can the chaste and pure lady of love for Kṛṣṇa touch it? Therefore, O mind, you should always serve the incomparable, beloved devotee commander of Kṛṣṇa's army, who will immediately throw out the unchaste woman and establish the pure lady of love in the heart.

* *Sādhu-premā* can mean: 1 love for *sādhus,* 2 the love that *sādhus* give to you, or 3 the love of Kṛṣṇa that *sādhus* help manifest in your heart. By using *premā,* a feminine form of *prema,* Raghunātha Dāsa Gosvāmī emphasizes the feminine nature of this love to contrast with the unchaste, dog-eating woman of desire for prestige.

The chaste ladies of pure spiritual love enter the heart when the desire for fame is removed.

VERSE EIGHT

यथा दुष्टत्वं मे दवयति शठस्यापि कृपया
यथा मह्यं प्रेमामृतमपि ददात्युज्ज्वलमसौ ।
यथा श्रीगान्धर्वाभजनविधये प्रेरयति मां
तथा गोष्ठे काक्वा गिरिधरमिह त्वं भज मनः ॥

yathā duṣṭatvaṁ me davayati śaṭhasyāpi kṛpayā
yathā mahyaṁ premāmṛtam api dadāty ujjvalam asau
yathā śrī-gāndharvā-bhajana-vidhaye prerayati māṁ
tathā goṣṭhe kākvā giridharam iha tvaṁ bhaja manaḥ

śaṭhasya-api—even though [I am] a cheater; *yathā*—so that; *kṛpayā*—by [his] mercy; *duṣṭatvaṁ me*—my inherent wickedness; *davayati*—is driven away; *yathā*—so that; *ujjvalam*—the glowing; *prema-amṛtam*—nectar of *prema*; *api*—is also; *dadāti*—bestowed completely; *mahyam*—on me; *yathā*—so that; *asau*—these; *śrī-gāndharvā-bhajana-vidhaye*—injunctions regarding worship of Śrī Gāndharvikā; *prerayati*—are inspired; *mām*—in my heart; *tathā*—for that purpose; *manaḥ*—O mind; *kākvā*—with pleading words; *tvaṁ bhaja*—you should worship; *giridharam*—Śrī Giridhārī, the lifter of Govardhana Hill; *iha*—here; *goṣṭhe*—in the land of cows, Vṛndāvana.

Even though I am a cheater, the Lord's mercy can drive away my inherent wicked nature, give me the glowing nectar of divine love, and inspire my heart with the process to worship Śrī Gāndharvikā. Therefore, O mind, with pleading words, you should worship Śrī Giridhārī here in Vṛndāvana.

Śrī Giridhārī engages the devotee in the worship of Śrī Gāndharvikā.

VERSE NINE

मदीशानाथत्वे व्रजविपिनचन्द्रं व्रजवने
श्वरीं तन्नाथत्वे तदतुलसखीत्वे तु ललिताम् ।
विशाखां शिक्षालीवितरणगुरुत्वे प्रियसरो
गिरीन्द्रौ तत्प्रेक्षाललितरतिदत्वे स्मर मनः ॥

mad-īśā-nāthatve vraja-vipina-candraṁ vraja-vane-
śvarīṁ tan-nāthatve tad-atula-sakhītve tu lalitām
viśākhāṁ śikṣālī-vitaraṇa-gurutve priyasaro-
girīndrau tat-prekṣā-lalita-rati-datve smara manaḥ

smara manaḥ—O mind, meditate on; *vraja-vipina-candram*—Kṛṣṇa, the moon of the Vṛndāvana forest; *mad-īśā-nāthatve*—as the lord of my controller or leader [Śrī Rādhikā]; *vraja-vana-īśvarīm*—Śrī Rādhā, the queen of the Vraja forest; *tan-nāthatve*—as his dearest object of love; *tu lalitām*—and Lalitā; *tad-atula-sakhītve*—as the incomparable friend; *viśākhām*—Viśākhā; *śikṣālī-vitaraṇa-gurutve*—as the foremost guru distributing the teachings of love; *priya-saraḥ-giri-indrau*—Rādhā-kuṇḍa and Govardhana; *tat-prekṣā-lalita-rati-datve*—as givers of the sight and love of Śrī Śrī Rādhā-Kṛṣṇa.

O mind, meditate on Kṛṣṇa, the moon of the Vṛndāvana forest, as the lord of my leader, Śrī Rādhikā. Meditate on Śrī Rādhikā as his most dear object of love. Meditate on Śrī Lalitā as her incomparable friend. Meditate on Śrī Viśākhā as the foremost guru distributing the teachings of love. And meditate on Rādhā-kuṇḍa and Govardhana as givers of the sight and love of Śrī Śrī Rādhā-Kṛṣṇa.

A forest goddess serves Kṛṣṇa, Śrī Rādhikā, Śrī Lalitā, and Śrī Viśākhā. This *līlā* is described in the *Ānanda-vṛndāvana-campū* of Kavi-karṇapūra.

VERSE TEN

रतिं गौरीलीले अपि तपति सौन्दर्यकिरणैः
शचीलक्ष्मीसत्याः परिभवति सौभाग्यवलनैः ।
वशीकारैश्चन्द्रावलिमुखनवीनव्रजसतीः
क्षिपत्याराद्या तां हरिदयितराधां भज मनः ॥

ratiṁ gaurī-līle api tapati saundarya-kiraṇaiḥ
śacī-lakṣmī-satyāḥ paribhavati saubhāgya-valanaiḥ
vaśīkārais candrāvali-mukha-navīna-vraja-satīḥ
kṣipaty ārād yā tāṁ hari-dayita-rādhāṁ bhaja manaḥ

bhaja manaḥ—offer worship, O mind; *tām*—unto her; *hari-dayita-rādhām*—Śrī Rādhā, the beloved of Lord Hari; *tapati*—[who] blazes; *ratim*—Rati [the wife of Kāmadeva]; *gaurī-līle api*—as well as Gaurī [the wife of Lord Śiva] and Līlā [the potency of Lord Viṣṇu]; *saundarya-kiraṇaiḥ*—by the effulgence of her beauty; *paribhavati*—[who] defeats; *śacī-lakṣmī-satyāḥ*—Śacī [the wife of Indra], Lakṣmī, and Satyā [Kṛṣṇa's wife]; *saubhāgya-valanaiḥ*—by the waves of her good fortune; *yā*—she who; *ārāt*—immediately; *kṣipati*—defeats; *navīna-vraja-satīḥ*—the newly married *gopīs* of Vraja; *candrāvali-mukha*—headed by Candrāvalī; *vaśīkāraiḥ*—through her power to control [Kṛṣṇa].

O mind, offer your worship unto Śrī Rādhikā, the beloved of Lord Hari. She outshines Rati [the wife of Kāmadeva], Gaurī [the wife of Lord Śiva], and Līlā [the potency of Lord Viṣṇu] by the effulgence of her beauty. She defeats Śacī [the wife of Indra], Lakṣmī, and Satyā [Kṛṣṇa's wife] by the waves of her good fortune. She defeats the pride of the newly married *gopīs* of Vraja, headed by Candrāvalī, through her power to control Kṛṣṇa.

Rādhārāṇī defeats the pride of the *gopīs* of Vraja. This *līlā* is described in *Śrīmad-Bhāgavatam* 10.32.4-8.

VERSE ELEVEN

समं श्रीरूपेण स्मरविवशराधागिरिभृतोर्
व्रजे साक्षात्सेवालभनविधये तद्गणयुजोः ।
तदिज्याख्याध्यानश्रवणनतिपञ्चामृतमिदं
धयन् नीत्या गोवर्धनमनुदिनं त्वं भज मनः ॥

samaṁ śrī-rūpeṇa smara-vivaśa-rādhā-giri-bhṛtor
vraje sākṣāt-sevā-labhana-vidhaye tad-gaṇa-yujoḥ
tad-ijyākhyā-dhyāna-śravaṇa-nati-pañcāmṛtam idaṁ
dhayan nītyā govardhanam anudinaṁ tvaṁ bhaja manaḥ

manaḥ—O mind; *anu-dinam*—every day; *dhayan*—drink; *idam*—this; *pañca-amṛtam*—five nectars; *tad-ijyākhyā-dhyāna-śravaṇa-nati*—the worship (*ijyā*), glories (*ākhyā*), meditation (*dhyāna*), listening of pastimes (*śravaṇa*) and offering obeisances (*nati*); *tvaṁ bhaja*—you should worship; *govardhanam*—Govardhana; *nītyā*—following the rules; *samam*—same as; *śrī-rūpeṇa*—Śrī Rūpa; *sākṣāt-sevā-labhana-vidhaye*—to obtain the means of direct service; *smara-vivaśa-rādhā-giri-bhṛtoḥ*—[of] Śrī Śrī Rādhā-Giridhārī, who are captivated by god of love; *tad-gaṇa-yujoḥ*—and associates; *vraje*—in Vraja.

O mind, you should every day drink the five nectars—worship, glories, meditation, listening to divine pastimes, and offering obeisances—and worship Govardhana according to the rules. In this way, follow the instructions of Śrī Rūpa and obtain the direct service of Śrī Śrī Rādhā-Giridhārī, who are captivated by the god of amourous love, in the company of their associates in Vraja.

Śrī Caitanya Mahāprabhu, the moon of the sky-like heart of devotees, personally gave his *govardhana-śilā* to Raghunātha Dāsa Gosvāmī.

VERSE TWELVE

मनःशिक्षादैकादशकवरमेतन् मधुरया
गिरा गायत्युच्चैः समधिगतसर्वार्थतति यः ।
सयूथः श्रीरूपानुग इह भवन् गोकुलवने
जनो राधाकृष्णातुलभजनरत्नं स लभते ॥

manaḥ-śikṣā-daikādaśaka-varam etan madhurayā
girā gāyaty uccaiḥ samadhigata-sarvārtha-tati yaḥ
sa-yūthaḥ śrī-rūpānuga iha bhavan gokula-vane
jano rādhā-kṛṣṇātula-bhajana-ratnaṁ sa labhate

śrī-rūpa-anuga bhavan—becoming a servant of Śrī Rūpa; *sa-yūthaḥ*—along with Rūpa's companions; *yaḥ*—one who; *madhurayā girā*—in a sweet voice; *gāyati uccaiḥ*—sings loudly; *etat*—these; *manaḥ-śikṣā-da-ekādaśaka-varam*—eleven supreme verses that give instructions to the mind; *samadhigata-sarva-artha-tati*—strives to understand all of their meanings completely; *janaḥ*—that person; *sa labhate*—obtains; *rādhā-kṛṣṇa-atula-bhajana-ratnam*—the incomparable jewel of worship of Śrī Śrī Rādha-Kṛṣṇa; *iha gokula-vane*—here in the Gokula forest.

Becoming a follower of Śrī Rūpa and his companions, one who with a sweet voice loudly recites these eleven supreme verses, which give instructions to the mind, and strives to understand all of their meanings completely, obtains the incomparable jewel of worshiping Śrī Śrī Rādhā-Kṛṣṇa in the forests of Gokula.

One who sweetly sings these verses obtains the incredible jewel of the service and worship of Śrī Śrī Rādhā-Kṛṣṇa.

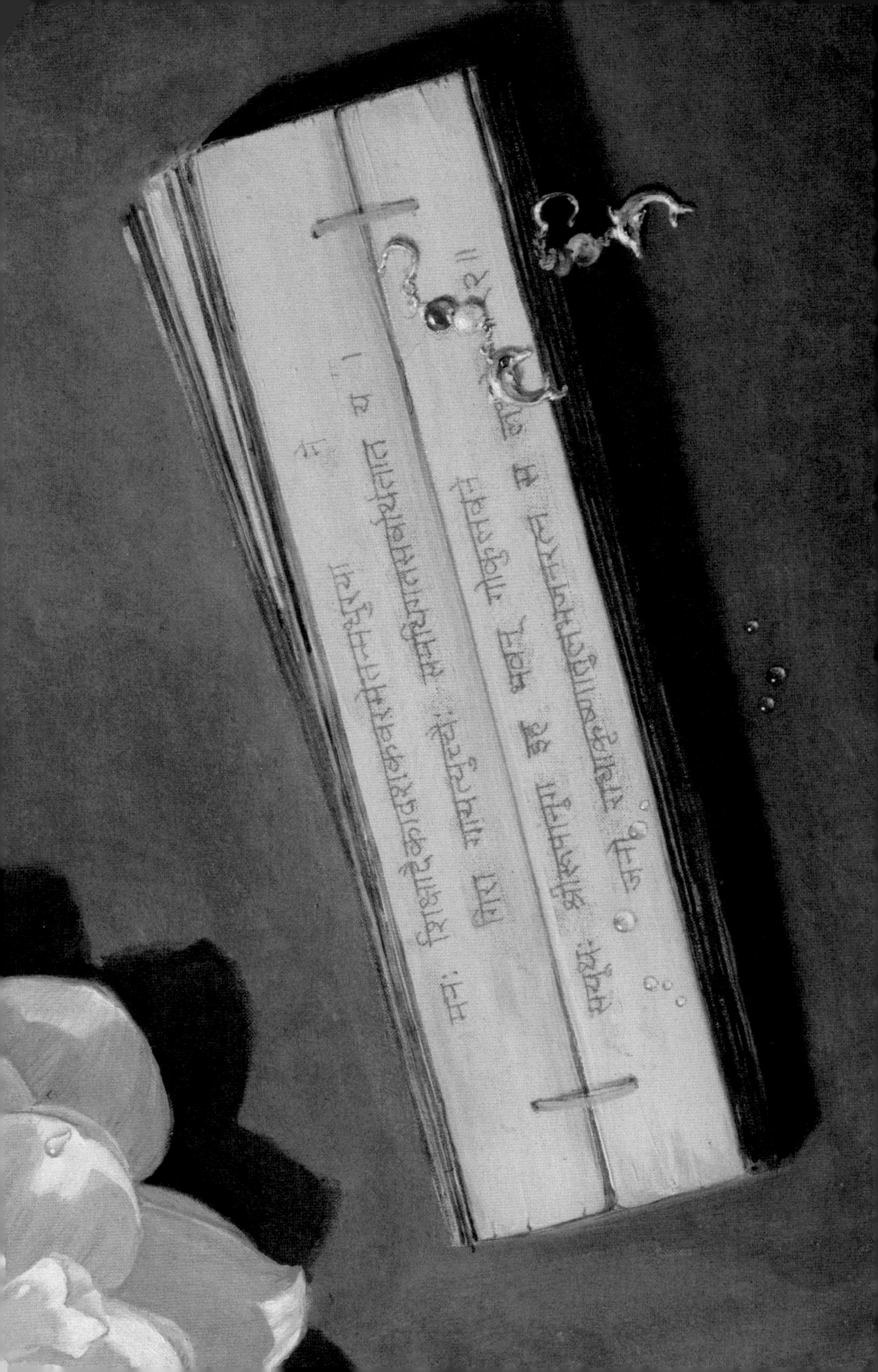

1 gurau goṣṭhe goṣṭhālayiṣu sujane bhū-sura-gaṇe
sva-mantre śrī-nāmni vraja-nava-yuva-dvandva-śaraṇe
sadā dambhaṁ hitvā kuru ratim apūrvām atitarāṁ
aye svāntar bhrātaś caṭubhir abhiyāce dhṛta-padaḥ

2 na dharmaṁ nādharmaṁ śruti-gaṇa-niruktaṁ kila kuru
vraje rādhā-kṛṣṇa-pracura-paricaryām iha tanu
śacī-sūnuṁ nandīśvara-pati-sutatve guru-varaṁ
mukunda-preṣṭhatve smara param ajasraṁ nanu manaḥ

3 yadīccher āvāsaṁ vraja-bhuvi sa-rāgaṁ pratijanur
yuva-dvandvaṁ tac cet paricaritum ārād abhilaṣeḥ
svarūpaṁ śrī-rūpaṁ sa-gaṇam iha tasyāgrajam api
sphuṭaṁ premṇā nityaṁ smara nama tadā tvaṁ śṛṇu manaḥ

4 asad-vārtā-veśyā visṛja mati-sarvasva-haraṇīḥ
kathā mukti-vyāghryā na śṛṇu kila sarvātma-gilanīḥ
api tyaktvā lakṣmī-pati-ratim ito vyoma-nayanīṁ
vraje rādhā-kṛṣṇau sva-rati-maṇidau tvaṁ bhaja manaḥ

5 asac-ceṣṭā-kaṣṭa-prada-vikaṭa-pāśālibhir iha
prakāmaṁ kāmādi-prakaṭa-patha-pāti-vyatikaraiḥ
gale baddhvā hanye 'ham iti bakabhid-vartmapa-gaṇe
kuru tvaṁ phutkārān avati sa yathā tvāṁ mana itaḥ

6 are cetaḥ prodyat-kapaṭa-kuṭināṭī-bhara-khara-
kṣaran-mūtre snātvā dahasi katham ātmānam api mām
sadā tvaṁ gāndharvā-giridhara-pada-prema-vilasat-
sudhāmbhodhau snātvā tvam api nitarāṁ māṁ ca sukhaya

1 O dear brother! O mind! Having given up all pride, please develop unprecedented and excessive attachment to Śrī Guru; to Śrī Vṛndāvana, the abode of cows; to the devotee residents of Vṛndāvana; to all the devotees on this planet; to the confidential mantra [given by Śrī Guru]; to the holy names of Śrī Śrī Rādhā-Kṛṣṇa; and to the process of surrendering to the fresh youthful couple of Vraja. Holding your feet, I beseech you with sweet words.

2 Indeed, do not perform any pious acts prescribed in the Vedas and supporting literature, or sinful acts forbidden in them. Staying here in Vraja, please perform profuse service to Śrī Śrī Rādhā-Kṛṣṇa. O mind, unceasingly remember the son of Śacī as the son of Nanda Mahārāja, and Śrī Guru as the dearest servant of Lord Mukunda.

3 Listen, O mind. If you desire, in every birth, to reside in the land of Vraja with loving attachment and to serve the youthful couple Śrī Śrī Rādhā-Kṛṣṇa in close proximity, then clearly remember and offer obeisances to Śrī Svarūpa, to Śrī Rūpa and his associates in Vṛndāvana, and to Śrī Rūpa's elder brother, Śrī Sanātana.

4 O mind, abandon the prostitute of mundane talks, who plunders all intelligence. Do not listen at all to the stories of the tigress named *mukti* (liberation), who devours all souls. Moreover, also give up attachment to the husband of Lakṣmī, Śrī Nārāyaṇa, who only leads one to Vaikuṇṭha. Instead, here in Vraja, serve Śrī Śrī Rādha-Kṛṣṇa, who give one the jewel of their own love.

5 "While here on the revealed path of devotion, I have been attacked by the gang of my own lust, etc., who have bound my neck with the troublesome dreadful ropes of wicked deeds. I am being killed!" Cry out piteously like this to the devotees of Śrī Kṛṣṇa, the destroyer of Baka. O mind, they will save you from these enemies.

6 O ruffian mind! Why do you burn yourself and me [the soul] by bathing in the trickling urine of the great donkey of full-blown hypocrisy and duplicity? Instead, you should always bathe in the ocean of love emanating from the lotus feet of Śrī Śrī Gāndharvikā-Giridhārī, thereby delighting yourself and me.

7 pratiṣṭhāśā dhṛṣṭā śvapaca-ramaṇī me hṛdi naṭet
kathaṁ sādhu-premā spṛśati śucir etan nanu manaḥ
sadā tvaṁ sevasva prabhu-dayita-sāmantam atulaṁ
yathā tāṁ niṣkāśya tvaritam iha taṁ veśayati saḥ

8 yathā duṣṭatvaṁ me davayati śaṭhasyāpi kṛpayā
yathā mahyaṁ premāmṛtam api dadāty ujjvalam asau
yathā śrī-gāndharvā-bhajana-vidhaye prerayati māṁ
tathā goṣṭhe kākvā giridharam iha tvaṁ bhaja manaḥ

9 mad-īśā-nāthatve vraja-vipina-candraṁ vraja-vane-
śvarīṁ tan-nāthatve tad-atula-sakhītve tu lalitām
viśākhāṁ śikṣālī-vitaraṇa-gurutve priyasaro-
girīndrau tat-prekṣā-lalita-ratidatve smara manaḥ

10 ratiṁ gaurī-līle api tapati saundarya-kiraṇaiḥ
śacī-lakṣmī-satyāḥ paribhavati saubhāgya-valanaiḥ
vaśīkāraiś candrāvali-mukha-navīna-vraja-satīḥ
kṣipaty ārād yā tāṁ hari-dayita-rādhāṁ bhaja manaḥ

11 samaṁ śrī-rūpeṇa smara-vivaśa-rādhā-giri-bhṛtor
vraje sākṣāt-sevā-labhana-vidhaye tad-gaṇa-yujoḥ
tad-ijyākhyā-dhyāna-śravaṇa-nati-pañcāmṛtam idaṁ
dhayan nītyā govardhanam anudinaṁ tvaṁ bhaja manaḥ

12 manaḥ-śikṣādaikādaśaka-varam etan madhurayā
girā gāyaty uccaiḥ samadhigata-sarvārtha-tati yaḥ
sa-yūthaḥ śrī-rūpānuga iha bhavan gokula-vane
jano rādhā-kṛṣṇātula-bhajana-ratnaṁ sa labhate

7 As long as the unchaste, dog-eating woman of desire for prestige dances in my heart, how can the chaste and pure lady of love for Kṛṣṇa touch it? Therefore, O mind, you should always serve the incomparable, beloved devotee commander of Kṛṣṇa's army, who will immediately throw out the unchaste woman and establish the pure lady of love in the heart.

8 Even though I am a cheater, the Lord's mercy can drive away my inherent wicked nature, give me the glowing nectar of divine love, and inspire my heart with the process to worship Śrī Gāndharvikā. Therefore, O mind, with pleading words, you should worship Śrī Giridhārī here in Vṛndāvana.

9 O mind, meditate on Kṛṣṇa, the moon of the Vṛndāvana forest, as the lord of my leader, Śrī Rādhikā. Meditate on Śrī Rādhikā as his most dear object of love. Meditate on Śrī Lalitā as her incomparable friend. Meditate on Śrī Viśākhā as the foremost guru distributing the teachings of love. And meditate on Rādhā-kuṇḍa and Govardhana as givers of the sight and love of Śrī Śrī Rādhā-Kṛṣṇa.

10 O mind, offer your worship unto Śrī Rādhikā, the beloved of Lord Hari. She outshines Rati [the wife of Kāmadeva], Gaurī [the wife of Lord Śiva], and Līlā [the potency of Lord Viṣṇu] by the effulgence of her beauty. She defeats Śacī [the wife of Indra], Lakṣmī, and Satyā [Kṛṣṇa's wife] by the waves of her good fortune. She defeats the pride of the newly married *gopīs* of Vraja, headed by Candrāvalī, through her power to control Kṛṣṇa.

11 O mind, you should every day drink the five nectars – worship, glories, meditation, listening to divine pastimes, and offering obeisances – and worship Govardhana according to the rules. In this way, follow the instructions of Śrī Rūpa and obtain the direct service of Śrī Śrī Rādhā-Giridhārī, who are captivated by the god of amourous love, in the company of their associates in Vraja.

12 Becoming a follower of Śrī Rūpa and his companions, one who with a sweet voice loudly recites these eleven supreme verses, which give instructions to the mind, and strives to understand all of their meanings completely, obtains the incomparable jewel of worshiping Śrī Śrī Rādhā-Kṛṣṇa in the forests of Gokula.

ABOUT THE ILLUSTRATIONS

VERSE 1 – NANDAGRĀMA

In this verse, we are instructed to love Vṛndāvana and its residents. This painting is of Nandagrāma, the area of Vṛndāvana where Kṛṣṇa's father and mother live. The painting is based on *Ānanda-vṛndāvana-campū* of Kavi-karṇapūra, chapter one. The following is a summary of relevant excerpts from that chapter.

Atop Nandīśvara Hill rests the splendid capital of Nanda. A high insurmountable wall appearing like the glow of the dawn surrounds all the smaller towns that comprise Nanda Mahārāja's capital. The main gateways are huge, jewel-studded doors. These towns appear like festive arenas with canopies and colorful jeweled festoons hanging from the archways. Nandīśvara is full of broad sparkling roadways. The many small, attractive temples appear as radiant as the rising sun. Their brilliant golden rooftops rival the splendorous yellow cloth of Lord Nārāyaṇa. Beautiful strands of pearls hang from the eaves. The golden rooftops, coral pillars, crystal walls, cat's eye towers, sapphire sitting platforms, and huge doors studded with large blue sapphires astound the eye with their beauty.

Nanda Mahārāja, the king of Vṛndāvana, resides in this town as the embodiment of paternal affection. His wife Yaśodā resides there as the embodiment of maternal affection, acting like a desire creeper which offers the *darśana* of Kṛṣṇa. Hundreds of honest and gentle cowherd families live in this capital city. The husbands embody religious principles and the wives embody devotional feelings. Their sons are Kṛṣṇa's cowherd boyfriends and their daughters are his dearest lovers. Like the four Kumāras, all of Kṛṣṇa's friends are eternally youthful. As flocks of birds decorate a forest, Kṛṣṇa is surrounded by friends of the same age. Kṛṣṇa and his friends have a very close and intimate relationship.

The delicate feet of Kṛṣṇa's *gopīs* resemble poetry full of wonderful rhymes. Their slender ankles move with the speed of the mind. The *gopīs'* faces are tenderly wiped by the fingers of Kṛṣṇa. Their noses surpass the beauty of sesame flowers whose fragrance enhances the elegance of spring. Their captivating lotus eyes resemble the merciful glance of the Lord blessing the world. With their beautiful ears they always drink the sweet nectar of *hari-kathā*.

All the *brāhmaṇas* living in Nanda's capital embody the principles of *bhāgavata-dharma*. They are extremely merciful and always display sense and mind control, tolerance, and renunciation. With great skill they recite *śāstras* like the *Śrīmad-Bhāgavatam*, and always study the *Nārada-pañcarātra* and other Vedic works that corroborate the *Bhāgavatam*. They alone qualify for Nanda Mahārāja's charity, and only they perform the appropriate rituals and ceremonies.

Although the oil sellers, *tāmbūla* salesmen, goldsmiths, pot makers, weavers, and blacksmiths have spiritual forms, they behave like ordinary humans. Commanding the respect of all pious men, they freely distribute their wealth wherever needed. They do not have material bodies, nor do they experience the sufferings of ordinary mortals.

Rows of huge *gośālās* spread out in all directions in Nanda Mahārāja's capital. The four long crystal walls of these *gośālās* are topped with emerald beams, and golden crossbeams that extend beyond the walls. In all corners ruby cornices are attached to the emerald beams. These *gośālās* are devoid of pillars and are very clean and expansive. Standing in the yards of the *gośālās* are the best of cows, which are as white as the full moon and have horns as dark as peaks of blue sapphires. These cows' thick bushy tails resemble the long hair of the ladies of Vṛndāvana. On seeing Kṛṣṇa, the cows are overwhelmed with joy and lift up their tails. There are also huge bulls that look like crystal boulders or big waves in an ocean of yogurt. Sleeping peacefully in their pens, they look like ancient sages in meditation. Like liberated souls, they freely wander here and there. Their huge horns resemble the tusks of the directional elephants. The high humps on their backs resemble the parasol and fans held above a king. With their red eyes and slow movements, they appear stunned.

Surrounding the town are many rows of small forest groves filled with varieties of multi-hued trees. With their many dangling creepers, the forests please the birds by providing playgrounds for their pastimes. The forest nymphs wander along the paths softened from the sap constantly dripping from the trees. An abundance of roots, herbs, and delicious fruits await the eager hands of the carefree cowherd boys. Lakes full of crystal clear water covered with water lilies, and white, blue and red lotuses are scattered throughout these forests.

VERSE 2 – LOVE IN THE STORM

In this verse, we are told to serve Rādhā and Kṛṣṇa. Kṛṣṇa in this verse is also called *nandīśvara-pati-sutatve,* meaning the son of Nanda who is the ruler of Vṛndāvana. In this painting we see Rādhā with Nanda and Kṛṣṇa. The painting is based on the *līlā* described in the *Brahma-vaivarta Purāṇa,* canto four. The following is a summary excerpt.

One day, taking infant Kṛṣṇa with him, Nanda tended the cows in a banyan grove of Vṛndāvana forest, holding infant Kṛṣṇa to his chest. Seeing the cloud-covered sky, darkened forest, howling winds, ferocious thunder, great rainstorm, wildly shaking trees, and falling branches, Nanda said, "How can I go home now and leave the calves behind? If I do not go home, what will become of my boy?" Seeing Rādhā as a youthful forest goddess, illuminating the ten directions with a splendor greater than ten million suns, suddenly come to that secluded place, Nanda said to her, "O beautiful one, now you may take my son and enjoy with him as you like. When your desires are all fulfilled, you will return him to me." After speaking these words, he fearfully gave the crying infant to her. She accepted him with a sweet and happy smile.

She held infant Kṛṣṇa to her heart's content, embracing him for a long time in her arms. She remembered the circle of the *rāsa* dance. Then Rādhā suddenly saw a palace with a hundred jewel domes and happily entered it. There she saw [infant Kṛṣṇa, in his form as] the handsome, dark, and youthfully fully grown Supreme Personality of Godhead, who was anointed with sandalwood paste and was splendid and playful. He said, "O Rādhā, O girl with the beautiful face, I love you more than anyone. You are identical with me. We are not different. When you do not stand by my side, people call me Kṛṣṇa. When you do stand by my side people call me splendid Kṛṣṇa (Śrī Kṛṣṇa)."

At that moment the demigod Brahmā came to that palace, carrying a garland and a *kamaṇḍalu* in his hands, and his four faces gently smiling. Brahmā first approached Śrī Kṛṣṇa, bowing down and offering prayers. Then he bowed his head before the lotus feet of Śrī Rādhā, the mother of all. With great respect he washed her feet with water from his *kamaṇḍalu* and then dried them with his hair. Folding his hands, he spoke many prayers.

Sitting between them, Brahmā ignited a sacred fire and, meditating on Lord Kṛṣṇa, properly offered oblations. He had Rādhā circumambulate Kṛṣṇa seven times and then circumambulate the fire. He had Kṛṣṇa take Rādhā's hand and recite seven Vedic mantras. Then grandfather Brahmā, the knower of the Vedas, placed Rādhā's hand on Kṛṣṇa's chest and Kṛṣṇa's hand on Rādhā's back and had Rādhā recite the Vedic mantras. Brahmā then had Rādhā place a knee-length *pārijāta* garland around Kṛṣṇa's neck and had Kṛṣṇa place a beautiful garland around Rādhā's neck. As if he were the father and she were his daughter, Brahmā gave Rādhā to Kṛṣṇa. The demigods showered *pārijāta* flowers, the Gandharvas sang, and the Apsarās danced. After the demigods left, Rādhā and Kṛṣṇa enjoyed loving pastimes.

After some time, Lord Kṛṣṇa abandoned the form of her youthful lover and became an infant again. Rādhā placed the infant Kṛṣṇa on her lap and gazed at the jewel palace, the flower garden, and the forest. Then, traveling as fast as the mind, she left the forest and arrived in half an eye blink at Nanda's palace.

As she was about to give the infant to Yaśodā, Rādhā sweetly said, "I had to endure many difficulties on the path as I tried to carry this very big, hungry, crying child your husband gave to me in the cow-pasture. O Yaśodā, the sky was filled with clouds, it rained again and again, and the path was muddy and almost impassable. My clothes were ruined. It was very difficult to carry your child. O saintly Yaśodā, please take your boy, give him your breast, and make him happy. I have been gone from home for a long time. I must return at once."

This *līlā* is also alluded to in Prabodhānanda Sarasvatī's commentary to *Gīta-govinda, Sāmoda-dāmodaraḥ*, verse 1: "Nanda said, 'O Rādha! Take this boy home. He is trembling. It is night. The sky is dense with rain clouds and the forest ground is dark because of the *tamāla* trees.' The private pastimes of Rādhā and Mādhava, who leave the forest on Nanda's order, exist eternally on the bank of the Yamunā with its paths, groves and trees."

VERSE 3 – KṚṢṆA AND BALARĀMA TAKE OUT THE CALVES

In this verse, Raghunātha Dāsa Gosvāmī instructs us to have *sa-rāgam*, or divine loving attachment. In his commentary on this verse, Bhaktivinoda quotes *Bhakti-rasāmṛta-sindhu* 1.2.292. Śrīla Prabhupāda translates this verse as follows where it appears in *Caitanya-caritāmṛta, Madhya-līlā* 22.155.

> When an advanced, realized devotee hears about the affairs of the devotees of Vṛndāvana – in the mellows [*rasas*] of *śānta, dāsya, sakhya, vātsalya and mādhurya* – he becomes inclined in one of these ways, and his intelligence becomes attracted. Indeed, he begins to covet that particular type of devotion. When such covetousness is awakened, one's intelligence no longer depends on the instructions of *śāstra* [revealed scripture] or on logic and argument.

This painting includes the most prominent devotees in each of the five primary *rasas* and is based on the description from *Bṛhad-bhāgavatāmṛta* of Sanātana Gosvāmī, chapter 6, verses 157–189. The following is a summary excerpt.

The young *gopīs* waited a moment to wish Kṛṣṇa a happy journey to the forest, and Yaśodā performed her duties to make his journey auspicious. Although their hearts were tortured with the thought of being separated from him, the young *gopīs* sang splendid and auspicious songs. Yaśodā placed protective amulets and ornaments proper for the forest on the limbs of both her son and his elder brother. She arranged for elderly *brāhmaṇa* ladies and other ladies to offer blessings. She did everything to prepare for his journey.

Taking the lunch his mother had given, Kṛṣṇa set out with the cows in front and played his flute. All of his companions, leaving their own homes, assembled around him. Together they played many melodies, on bamboo flutes, horn bugles, and leaf flutes. Kṛṣṇa's friends carried paraphernalia for his pastimes and happily sang, danced, and spoke words of praise.

Yaśodā, milk flowing from her breasts, followed him outside the gates. Kṛṣṇa spoke to her, and she turned to go home. Turning her neck to see him, she took two or three steps and then, overcome, went again to her son. She prepared some betel nuts and placed them in his hand and mouth. She again turned to go and, as before, quickly came back to him. In the middle of the road she fed her son sweets mixed with fruit and gave him something to drink. Then she began to go home again but returned as before. Carefully inspecting her son's garments and other things, she set everything neatly in order. Again she left and returned. She instructed her son, "Son, don't go far in this impassable forest, and never go where there are thorns." With many sweet words she made him promise. Then she turned to go, took a few steps, and returned again. "Dear Balarāma, you stay in front of your younger brother. Śrīdāmā, you stay with Sarūpa in the rear. Aṁśu, you stay at his right. Subala, you stay at his left." With a blade of grass, she begged them. Then she gazed at her son. With an agitated heart, coming and going again and again, her affection defeated that of a *surabhi* cow for her new-born calf.

As Kṛṣṇa left for the forest, the *gopīs,* pulled by the rope of love and unable to bear separation from him, began to follow behind. With shyness and fear, they were unable to say or do anything. Their eyes flooded with streams of tears and they stumbled, drowning in an ocean of pain without any remedy. Kṛṣṇa charmed the eyes and hearts of these girls, who had come very far from Vraja village. With a great effort he made them return home, although again and again he glanced at them as they left. With an anxious heart he turned his neck and again comforted them with his glances of love. The movements of his eyebrows, which carried the message of his love, embarrassed them. Stunned, they stood next to his mother, Yaśodā.

Nanda Mahārāja, the king of the *gopas,* seeing his wife's love for her son, also became filled with love. Accompanied by the adult *gopas,* he followed Kṛṣṇa for a long way and could not give him up. Seeing many auspicious omens and seeing that the cows and other creatures were very happy, Nanda was happy at heart, but he was also tormented by the thought of separation from his son. He embraced his older son, Balarāma, then embraced his younger son, Kṛṣṇa, and then embraced both of them again and again. He smelled their heads and cried, overcome with love. Kṛṣṇa bowed down before him and explained all the duties to be done. Nanda gazed at his son and stood still and motionless.

When he saw his two sons were deep in the forest and he could no longer hear any sounds from them, he turned towards Vraja village. Sending some swift servant-messengers to bring news of the boys, he comforted his wife and the *gopīs* and brought them all to their homes.

VERSE 4 – RĀDHĀ DECORATES KṚṢṆA'S HAIR

In this verse, Raghnunatha Dāsa Gosvāmī tells us to serve Rādha and Kṛṣṇa, who are the givers of the jewel of their own love. In this painting, Rādha decorates Kṛṣṇa with jewels of love. The picture is based on the following description from *Govinda-līlāmṛta,* chapter 15, verses 99–103.

After bathing, Kṛṣṇa's and the *sakhīs'* bodies and hair were wiped dry with fine cloth by their friends. They were then given upper and lower clothes. Then Kṛṣṇa and the *sakhīs,* along with Vṛndā and others, quickly arrived at the bower called the Lotus Pavilion. When Kṛṣṇa sat on a platform in the southern part of the bower, Rādhā decorated him with flower ornaments made with great skill. She dried and perfumed his hair with *aguru* incense, combed it and covered it with a jasmine garland.

In his hair she placed clusters of flowers, leaves, and peacock feathers. She wound his hair with garlands of flowers upward on his topknot, which was broad at the base and narrow at the top, and placed garlands on the sides. This attracted the bees, who appeared like *cāmara* whisks fanning Kṛṣṇa. His topknot attracted the bee-like eyes of the *gopīs* who could not detach themselves from it thereafter. And the topknot became attracted to the *gopīs'* hearts and could not leave them. Seeing the shadow of the topknot, even Kṛṣṇa became bewildered. The whole world fell under the control of this topknot.

VERSE 5 – PROTECTORS ON THE PATH OF *BHAKTI*

In this verse, Raghunātha Dāsa Gosvāmī tells us to ask for help from the devotees of Baka's killer, Kṛṣṇa, as we travel on the shining path of devotion. In his commentary to this verse, Bhaktivinoda Ṭhākura quotes the following prayer.

prahlāda-nārada-parāśara-puṇḍarīka-
vyāsāmbarīṣa-śuka-śaunaka-bhīṣma-dalbhyān
rukmāṅgadoddhava-vibhīṣaṇa-phālgunādīn
puṇyān imān parama-bhāgavatān namāmi

To the saintly devotees of the Lord, headed by Prahlāda, Nārada, Parāśara, Puṇḍarīka, Vyāsa, Ambarīṣa, Śuka, Śaunaka, Bhīṣma, Dalbhya, Rukmāṅgada, Uddhava, Vibhīṣaṇa, and Arjuna, I offer my respectful obeisances. (*Padyāvalī* 52)

The painting shows three of the persons in this prayer – Nārada, Bhīṣma, and Arjuna – as protectors on *bhakti's* shining path. *Śrīmad-Bhāgavatam* 10.84.57–58 describes how these three persons were together at Kurukṣetra during an extended period before and after a solar eclipse.

VERSE 6 – GĀNDHARVIKĀ-GIRIDHĀRĪ

Raghunātha Dāsa Gosvāmī instructs us in this verse to swim in the ocean of love at the feet of Gāndharvikā-Giridhārī. Because Gāndharvikā is a name for Rādhā that indicates her expertise in music, in this painting she is with her "stringed instrument known as a *kacchapī-vīṇā*, which is the fame and fortune that actually dries up the faces and breasts of the other *gopīs*." (*Caitanya caritāmṛta, Madhya-līlā* 8.166 purport). Since Kṛṣṇa is called Giridhārī, or the lifter of Govardhana Hill, this painting shows the divine couple at Govardhana. What follows are some references which inspired this painting.

Padyāvalī 191: "Rādhā taught her caged parrot to recite the words of your [Kṛṣṇa's] letter. She turned your letter into a song she sings to the accompaniment of flute and *vīṇā*." – Śrī Govardhanācārya.

Gītā Mālā 6 by Bhaktivinoda Ṭhākura: "Oh Rādhe! You are wildly exciting Kṛṣṇa's mind with your fragrant bodily aroma and the sweet sound of your *vīṇā*."

Dāna-keli-kaumudī of Rūpa Gosvāmī: "Kṛṣṇa says, 'Who is this girl? Standing by Govardhana Hill, moving the bows of her eyebrows, and shooting arrows of sidelong glances past her glistening jewel earrings, she wounds and bewilders me. Aha! Can this be my beloved, the dove who makes her nest in my heart? Now I have found my Rādhā, who is graceful, artistic, and passionately in love with me, whose graceful words decorate my ear, and who is like a *vīṇā* that makes graceful sweet sounds with ornaments of many notes and quarter-notes in the different ragas.'"

Kṛṣṇa-bhāvanāmṛta-mahākāvya by Viśvanātha Cakravartī Ṭhākura, chapter 19: "Rādhikā began to play her *vallakī vīṇā,* holding it in her lotus-like hands as Kṛṣṇa held his *haṁsīka* flute in his lotus-like hands. It was as if they wanted to defeat each other in expertise in singing and playing music! Their music turned water into stone and stone into water. That's quite normal, but even the hearts of the *munis* in Satyaloka, who were absorbed in non-dual vision, melted and poured down on earth. That was most amazing!" And in chapter 12: "Kṛṣṇa said, 'Rādhā, it is your *vīṇā* who defeated my *muralī* out of envy through all her artistry, who makes me happy with her sweetness and who has an ample breast (the gourd of the *vīṇā*) like yours!'"

VERSE 7 – THE CHASTE LADIES OF PURE LOVE

In this verse, Raghunātha Dāsa Gosvāmī tells us that when all desire for fame and honor is removed from our heart, the pure lady of spiritual love, *sādhu-premā,* can enter. It is significant that he uses the feminine form of the word rather than the more commonly used *prema*.

This painting shows the ultimate feminine expressions of love for Kṛṣṇa, the cowherd girls, decorating and dressing each other solely for Kṛṣṇa's pleasure, just as the *sādhu-premā* prepares our pure heart to welcome the Lord. Here are some summaries and excerpts from various sources upon which the painting is based.

Śrīla Prabhupāda's lecture on *The Nectar of Devotion* on November

12, 1972, in Vṛndāvana: "The *gopīs* used to dress themselves so that Kṛṣṇa will feel satisfied, satisfaction. For Kṛṣṇa's satisfaction. They used to dress for Kṛṣṇa's satisfaction. That is, of course, very difficult to understand. But we should learn from the *śāstras*. The *gopīs* had no sense gratification desire. They wanted to satisfy Kṛṣṇa."

Caitanya-caritāmṛta, Antya-līlā 18.101: "Then they [the *gopīs*] all bathed again, and after putting on dry clothing, they went to a small jeweled house, where the *gopī* Vṛndā arranged to dress them in forest clothing by decorating them with fragrant flowers, green leaves and all kinds of other ornaments."

Govinda-līlāmṛta 15.99, 108: "Everyone proceeded to the lotus temple in the southwest corner of Rādhā-kuṇḍa ... According to the season, the principal *gopīs* decorated Rādhā in different combinations of matching flowers. Afterwards, the attendants (*mañjarīs*) of the *gopīs* tastefully dressed them."

Caitanya-carita of Murāri Gupta, 10.16–25: "The *mañjarīs*, endowed with jewel-like attributes, enhanced the stunning beauty of Rādhā's limbs with ornaments made of flowers whose natural beauty surpassed the opulence of costly jewels. Some *gopīs* retied their braids after drying their hair. While holding mirrors in their right hands, the *gopīs* used their left hands to replace the scattered locks that had fallen over their foreheads. The dressing place seems to be the capital of Cupid. One *sakhī* looked superb with her unbound hair. Yet to display her artistry she had her *mañjarīs* skillfully tie it up. After dressing each other, the *sakhīs* happily approached Kṛṣṇa."

VERSE 8 — WORSHIP OF RĀDHĀ

In this verse, Raghunātha Dāsa Gosvāmī asks Kṛṣṇa, Śrī Giridhārī, for engagement in the worship of Rādhā, Gāndharvikā. The painting shows Kṛṣṇa bringing a *gopī* to Rādhārāṇī so the *gopī* can worship her and receive her shelter.

Śrīla Bhaktivinoda Ṭhākura sings, *rādhā bhajane yadi mati nāhi bhelā kṛṣṇa bhajana tava akārana gelā*: "If one is not inclined toward the worship of Rādhā, his worship of Kṛṣṇa is useless."

VERSE 9 – THE *GOPĪS* AND KṚṢṆA AT NIGHT

In this verse, Raghunātha Dāsa Gosvāmī has us meditate on Kṛṣṇa, Rādhā, Lalitā, and Viśākhā. This painting is of them in their nighttime pastimes and is based on the following description from *Ānanda-vṛndāvana-campū*, chapter 20.

Surrounding the supreme enjoyer and lord of their lives, who wore an elegant crown, a *kaustubha* necklace, and other effulgent ornaments, the *gopīs* entered the courtyards of the forest *kuñjas* along the Yamunā, which resounded with flocks of singing swans and other water birds. The *vanadevīs* (forest nymphs, fairies, and goddesses who are servants of Vṛndā-devī) provided delicious, fragrant *madhu* (a honey beverage made from flower extracts) in jeweled pitchers. Intoxicated by the fragrance, swarms of bees flew in from all directions and circled overhead. Though lit by the full moon, the evening sky appeared darkened by their presence. Illumined by the moonlight, the beach looked like a silver band and the crystal glasses looked enchanting. Because the moonlight and the crystal glasses glistened with equal intensity, one could distinguish them only by touch and not by sight.

VERSE 10 – KṚṢṆA RETURNS TO THE *RĀSA* DANCE

Raghunātha Dāsa Gosvāmī says in this verse that Rādhā defeats the pride of all the damsels of Vraja. This painting shows the eight principal *gopīs* greeting Kṛṣṇa after he returned to the *rāsa* dance. The following are descriptions of this *līlā* upon which the painting is based.

ŚRĪMAD-BHĀGAVATAM 10.32.4–8

When the *gopīs* saw that their dearmost Kṛṣṇa had returned to them, they all stood up at once, and out of their affection for him their eyes bloomed wide. It was as if the air of life had reentered their bodies. One *gopī* joyfully took Kṛṣṇa's hand between her folded palms, and another placed his arm, anointed with sandalwood paste, on her shoulder. A slender *gopī* respectfully took in her joined hands the betel nut he had chewed, and another *gopī*, burning with desire, put his lotus feet on her breasts. One *gopī*, beside herself with loving anger, bit her lips and stared at him with frowning eyebrows, as if to wound him with her harsh glances. Another *gopī* looked with unblinking eyes upon his lotus face, but even after deeply relishing its sweetness she did not feel satiated, just as mystic saints are never satiated when meditating upon the Lord's feet. One *gopī* took the Lord through the aperture of her eyes and placed him within her heart. Then, with her eyes closed and her bodily hairs standing on end, she continuously embraced him within. Thus immersed in transcendental ecstasy, she resembled a *yogī* meditating upon the Lord.

VIŚVANĀTHA CAKRAVARTĪ ṬHĀKURA'S COMMENTARY

Five verses describe the personal loving activities of some of the principal *gopīs*. One *gopī* held Kṛṣṇa's right hand in hers. This is understood because in the second half of the verse, it is described that another *gopī* put his other hand, decorated with sandalwood pictures, on her shoulder. That would be his left hand, since it is proper from the *gopīs* to stand to the left of Kṛṣṇa. The *gopī* took his hand out of courteous friendship and explicit eagerness. Because of the reverential touch of the *gopī*, it can be understood that she was of the subservient group fully surrendered to Kṛṣṇa, thinking herself as belonging to Kṛṣṇa, with ghee-like love. Because she is mentioned first, it may be concluded that she was senior most of that group, Candrāvalī.

The other *gopī*, characterized by a slightly reverential embrace, was an independent lover with an explicit expression of affection, honey-like love mixed with ghee-like love. That *gopī* was Śyāmalā, a member of the group friendly to Rādhā.

One *gopī* took Kṛṣṇa's chewed *tāmbūla* in her folded hands. She was a member of the right-wing group, dependent, with friendship almost of the *dāsya* mood. Another *gopī* took Kṛṣṇa's right lotus foot and placed it on her breast, while sitting on the earth. Supporting himself with his left arm on the shoulder of a *gopī*, he was standing on his left foot. The seated *gopī* was of the right-wing group, dependent, with *dasya* almost of friendly mood. Both were in the mood of ghee-like love, thinking of themselves as belonging to Kṛṣṇa. These are *sakhīs* of Candrāvalī – Padmā and Śaibyā.

One *gopī*, arching her brows like a bow, helplessly subject to the anger of love, aimed arrow glances at Kṛṣṇa, as if to shoot him. "O leader of rogues! You have been completely successful in administering the *hālahala* poison of *prema* to me. Why are you again approaching me to burn my life airs which have almost left my body already? I can understand very well who you are." This was the mood she revealed as she glanced upon him. She bit her lips, hiding them with her hands as an expression of anger. This *gopī* exhibited jealousy arising from honey-like love, thinking of Kṛṣṇa as hers. This *gopī* was Rādhā.

One *gopī* gazed at Kṛṣṇa with unblinking eyes due to being stunned with bliss. Like bees mad to taste the lotus honey of his face, her two eyes, though relishing his face, were not satisfied. Or this can be interpreted in another way. Because of the fierce glance of Rādhā mentioned in the previous verse, Kṛṣṇa's face was trembling with fear and remorseful. Therefore, that *gopī* could not be satisfied, though tasting repeatedly that face relished by her two eyes.

Though Kṛṣṇa's face is an ocean of sweetness, at that time, because of the mixture of the *sañcārī bhāvas* such as shyness, despair, meekness and fear, because of being struck with the arrow glance of the leader of her group, the ocean of sweetness increased to the extreme with great variety. The *gopī* could not be satisfied because of her increased thirst.

For lacking a complete analogy (covering both interpretations) to illustrate this, one covering the first interpretation is given in the verse: Just as devotees situated in the *dāsya* and *sakhya bhāvas* cannot be completely satisfied though they serve Kṛṣṇa's lotus feet repeatedly, so this *gopī* also could not be satisfied.

It should be understood that Kṛṣṇa cast his full glance and full mind upon the previous *gopī* [Rādhā], who was glaring at him with furrowed brows, and did not divert himself to anyone else at all. So the *gopī* mentioned in this verse, seeing that Kṛṣṇa was inattentive towards her, looked at Kṛṣṇa with both eyes, directly, leisurely, and without shyness.

One *gopī*, understanding that Kṛṣṇa was fickle (even if he comes, he will go away again), took him into her heart. Thinking he would escape through her eye holes, she closed her eyes. Her body erupted in goosebumps because of the unobstructed enjoyment of union with Kṛṣṇa. She stood there in a pose of embracing Kṛṣṇa to her chest with her arms, her sense control being absent due to intense thirst at the end of long separation, and her shyness absent due to outsiders not gazing on her.

The *gopīs* mentioned in verses 6–8, because they did not go to the side of their beloved, are understood to be of the uncooperative type, or right-wing. They thought, "He should come to us; we should not go to him." From this mentality it can be understood that these three *gopīs*, being possessive and with honey-like love, were very intimate with Kṛṣṇa and brought him under their control. Among the three, the *gopī* mentioned in verse six is Rādhā, the leader of the best group. Those mentioned in verse seven and eight are her *sakhīs*. According to *Vaiṣṇava-toṣaṇī*, the *gopīs* mentioned in verses 4–8 are, respectively, Candrāvalī, Śyāmalā, Śaibyā, Padmā, Rādhā, Lalitā and Viśākhā. Bhadrā, the eighth *gopī* is mentioned in the Viṣṇu Purāṇa: "One *gopī* looking at Kṛṣṇa became joyful and began to sing his name repeatedly. She could say nothing else."

These eight *gopīs* are considered the best of all the *gopīs*, as explained in the *Dvārakā-māhātmya* in the *Prahlāda-saṁhitā* of the *Skanda Purāṇa*, quoted in *Vaiṣṇava-toṣaṇī*. To understand the ranking among those eight *gopīs* one should consult *Ujjvala-nīlamaṇi*. The chief of all the *gopīs* is Rādhā. The *Padmā Purāṇa* says, "As Rādhā is dear to Kṛṣṇa, so also is her *kuṇḍa*. Among all the *gopīs* she is unparalleled, the dearest to Kṛṣṇa." The *Bṛhad-gautamīya-tantra* says, "Śrī Rādhā is the most beautiful, always absorbed in Kṛṣṇa. She is the most worshipable supreme *devatā*, the abode of all *lakṣmīs*, fulfills all of Kṛṣṇa's desires, is the attractor of the mind of Kṛṣṇa, and is the full *śakti* of Kṛṣṇa. She is inseparable from Kṛṣṇa." The *Ṛk-pariśiṣṭa* says, "Mādhava with Rādhā and Rādhā with Mādhava are the most attractive thing in the whole universe."

GOPĀLA-CAMPŪ, CHAPTER 25

Kṛṣṇa became ashamed of having abandoned the *gopīs* and thus stood rather neutrally. The *gopīs* quickly ran from all sides to him, just as the rivers flow quickly and join the ocean when the ocean shrinks. Each *gopī* strove to be the first to meet him. The *gopī* who met him first was Bhadrā.

Candrāvalī held Kṛṣṇa's right hand in her hands, just as fresh leaves surround an excellent lotus. Padmā, by trickery, placed his lotus foot on her breasts, just as a woman puts a red lotus on the head of Śiva upon having her desires fulfilled. Śaibyā, situated to his right, a slender gopī, took his chewed betel nut in her palms, which appeared like the vessel holding attraction for him.

Śyāmalā, situated to his left, held Kṛṣṇa's arm, which was covered with sandalwood pulp, on her shoulder. She showed her competence by her affection and her bodily complexion. Lalitā bountifully drank the lotus face of Kṛṣṇa with her unblinking eyes, which resembled a pair of the best of bees. She relished his form. Her two eyes in tasting the honey surpassed a pair of bees. When Viśākhā saw Kṛṣṇa, her mind became filled with shame. She stood like a doll, with unblinking eyes and hairs standing on end. I feel astonished at this woman who met with her lover internally. In separation she attained him within, and at the end of great separation, she met with him continually.

How can one describe the *prema* of Rādhā? Situated in front of Kṛṣṇa, her *prema* spread anger, though uselessly, and her eyes, though motionless, became weapons that shot arrows from her position and gave pain to Kṛṣṇa though not injuring him. All of the women, just on meeting Kṛṣṇa, felt successful. Just as the *nava* plant blossoms in the presence of a dark cloud, the beauty of their faces blossomed on attaining Kṛṣṇa. They became joyful.

ĀNANDA-VṚNDĀVANA-CAMPŪ, CHAPTER 20

One *gopī* grasped Kṛṣṇa's lotus hands, another leading *gopī* placed his arms on her musk-scented shoulders, and one *gopī*, inclined to service, respectfully took his chewed betel in her hands, which served as a golden spittoon. One leading *gopī*, burning with desire, put his lotus foot on her budding breasts. Decorated with the fresh young leaves of his toes, her breasts looked like a pair of auspicious golden water pots announcing the upcoming *rāsa* dance.

Standing at a distance, one *gopī*, beside herself with loving anger, bit her beautiful lips and glared at him with frowning eyebrows. While casting glances from her reddened eyes smeared with *kājala*, it seemed as if she shot arrows tipped with the poison of pride. Another *gopī* with unblinking eyes drank the honey of his lotus face, but even after deeply relishing its sweetness she did not feel satiated. Only when Kṛṣṇa looked into her eyes did she become satisfied.

One married *gopī* took the Lord through the aperture of her eyes and placed him in the temple of her heart. Then fearing his departure, with her eyes closed and her bodily hairs standing on end, she continuously embraced him within.

VERSE 11 — LORD CAITANYA'S *GOVARDHANA-ŚILĀ*

Raghunātha Dāsa Gosvāmī in this verse instructs us to worship Govardhana. This painting shows him receiving a Govardhana stone [*śilā*] from the hand of Lord Caitanya. The following is a summary excerpt from *Caitanya caritāmṛta, Antya-līlā* 6.288–301, upon which the painting is based.

Śrī Caitanya Mahāprabhu bestowed his mercy upon Raghunātha Dāsa by giving him a stone from Govardhana Hill and a garland of small conchshells. Previously, Śaṅkarānanda Sarasvatī had given the Govardhana stone and the garland of conchshells to Śrī Caitanya Mahāprabhu, making Mahāprabhu extremely happy. While chanting, the Lord would put the garland around his neck. He would put the stone to his heart or sometimes to his eyes. Sometimes he would smell it and sometimes place it on his head. The Govardhan stone was always moist with tears from his eyes. Śrī Caitanya Mahāprabhu would say, "This stone is directly the body of Lord Kṛṣṇa."

For three years he kept the stone and garland. Then, greatly satisfied by the behavior of Raghunātha Dāsa, the Lord delivered both of them to him. Śrī Caitanya Mahāprabhu instructed Raghunātha Dāsa, "This stone is the transcendental form of Lord Kṛṣṇa. Worship the stone with great eagerness. Worship this stone in the mode of goodness like a perfect *brāhmaṇa*, for by such worship you will surely attain ecstatic love of Kṛṣṇa without delay. For such worship, one needs a jug of water and a few flowers from a Tulasī tree. This is worship in complete goodness when performed in complete purity. With faith and love, you should offer eight soft Tulasī flowers, each with two leaves, one on either side of each flower."

After thus advising him how to worship, Śrī Caitanya Mahāprabhu personally offered Raghunātha Dāsa the *govardhana-śilā* with his transcendental hand. As advised by the Lord, Raghunātha Dāsa worshiped the stone in great transcendental jubilation.

Svarūpa Dāmodara gave Raghunātha Dāsa two cloths, each about six inches long, a wooden platform, and a jug in which to keep water. Thus Raghunātha Dāsa began worshiping the Govardhana stone, and as he worshiped he saw the Supreme Personality of Godhead, Kṛṣṇa, the son of Nanda Mahārāja, directly in the stone. Thinking of how he had received the *govardhana-śilā* directly from the hands of Śrī Caitanya Mahāprabhu, Raghunātha Dāsa was always overflooded with ecstatic love.

VERSE 12 – A BENEDICTION

This benedictory verse assures us of attaining the jewel of love of God by reciting the verses sweetly and with understanding. The painting is of a leaf book, typical of the time and place in which Raghunātha Dāsa Gosvāmī lived. Verse twelve is shown written on the book in Devanagari letters. A lotus is included because it is commonly associated with Lord Kṛṣṇa. The jeweled earrings are of dolphins. Kṛṣṇa regularly wears earrings in the shape of dolphins, sharks, or *makaras,* a type of large aquatic creature.

DESCRIPTIONS OF KṚṢṆA'S ASSOCIATES

The following are descriptions from the *śāstra* of some of Kṛṣṇa's Vrṇdāvana associates depicted in the paintings, especially regarding their complexion and favored clothing.

- **Rādhārāṇī** – She is fourteen years old, has a golden complexion, and wears a deep blue cloth with a pink blouse and a red veil.
- **Lalitā** – She is fourteen years old, has golden yellow complexion,

and her clothes are the colors of a peacock's feathers. She often brings camphor and *tāmbūla* to Kṛṣṇa.

- **Viśākhā** – She is fourteen years old, her complexion is cream with a tinge of red, and her clothes are like clusters of stars in the evening sky. She brings clothes and cloth to Kṛṣṇa and often picks flowers.
- **Nanda Mahārāja** – He has a protuberant belly, his complexion is the color of sandalwood, he is tall and his garments are the color of a *bandhujīva* flower (green). His beard is a mixture of black and white hairs, like rice and toasted sesame seeds mixed together.
- **Yaśodā** – Her complexion is like the color of wheat, and her garments are like a rainbow. Yaśodā's body is of a medium size, neither large nor small. She has long black hair.
- **Subala** – He has a fair complexion, wears handsome blue clothes, and is decorated with many kinds of jewels and flowers. He is twelve years old and full of youthful luster. He is cheerful.
- **Ujjvala** – He has a splendid, dark reddish-brown complexion, his garments are decorated with star patterns, and he wears pearls and flowers. He is thirteen years old and full of youthful luster.
- **Śrīdāmā** – He wears yellow clothes, and his turban is a reddish copper color. His bodily complexion is blackish. He wears a nice garland around his neck and carries a buffalo horn.
- **Raktaka and Patraka** – These servants carry Kṛṣṇa's flutes, buffalo-horn bugle, stick, rope and other paraphernalia, such as the mineral dyes that the cowherd boys use to decorate their bodies.
- **Raktaka** – He wears yellow clothing, and his bodily color is just like newly grown grass. He is very expert in singing.
- **Śyāmalā** – She wears red cloth and plays a *vīṇā*.
- **Bhadrā** – She wears cloth decorated with pictures and plays a *vīṇā*.
- **Candrāvalī** – She is fifteen years old and wears blue cloth. She is extremely beautiful, second only to Rādhārāṇī.
- **Padmā** – She is fifteen years old and wears red cloth.
- **Śaibyā** – She is fifteen years old, wears red cloth, and plays a flute.

Some people who appear in the paintings, such as Rohiṇī and Patraka, are not described in the *śāstra* in regards to their complexion or favored clothing.

BIOGRAPHIES

RAGHUNĀTHA DĀSA GOSVĀMĪ, AUTHOR

Raghunātha Dāsa Gosvāmī (1495-1586) was born in a family of very wealthy landowners, and much hope rested on him to take over the family business. But at the age of nineteen, he left his family and traveled to Jagannātha Purī to take shelter of Lord Caitanya Mahāprabhu. Raghunātha Dāsa became Svarūpa Dāmodara Gosvāmī's assistant and received frequent personal association and instructions from Lord Caitanya. After the Lord left this world, Raghunātha Dāsa went to Vṛndāvana and received instructions from Rūpa Gosvāmī and Sanātana Gosvāmī. He lived near Rādhā-kuṇḍa for the rest of his life. He worked to find and restore different places of Lord Kṛṣṇa's pastimes in the area and wrote and compiled many important books, including *Stavāvalī, Śrī Vilāpa-kusumāñjali, Dāna-keli-cintāmaṇi, Muktā-carita,* and *Manaḥ-śikṣā*. Bhaktivinoda Ṭhākura has instructed, "*Śrī Manaḥ-śikṣā* has laid down a systematic procedure for one to enter into and become absorbed in the pastimes of Śrī Śrī Rādhā-Kṛṣṇa; one should follow it without guile."

HARI PĀRṢADA DĀSA, TRANSLATOR

Hari Pārṣada Dāsa is a disciple of H.H. Radha Govinda Dāsa Goswami Mahārāja, who is a disciple of A.C. Bhaktivedanta Swami Prabhupāda. He was born in a *gauḍa-sārasvatā-brāhmaṇa* family in Mumbai, Maharashtra, India. His father and grandfather are both devotees of Śrī Śrī Rukmiṇī Viṭṭhala of Pandharpur. Hari Pārṣada Dāsa learned Sanskrit grammar in the traditional way in his childhood and was taught the *Laghu-siddhānta-kaumudī* of Paṇḍita Varadarāja. Coming in contact with ISKCON in 2002, he dedicated himself to preaching to the youth in Mumbai. After rendering this service for five years, he started furthering his Sanskrit studies and studied the *Aṣṭādhyāyī,* the complete four thousand *sūtras* by Pāṇini. Because of his scholarly knowledge and Sanskrit translation skills, he was appointed as an assistant editor at Gopal Jiu Publications.

JÑĀNĀÑJANA DĀSA, ILLUSTRATOR

Born in 1955 at Terni, Italy as Tomassetti Giampaolo, Jñānāñjana Dāsa is one of the founders of the International Vedic Art Academy at Villa Vrindavana, Florence, Italy. He was part of the academy from 1980–87. Jñānāñjana's work often comes in large sizes and bold colors, featuring Kṛṣṇa epics. Several of his paintings have been used to illustrate books for the Bhaktivedanta Book Trust. He also makes mixed media art focusing on the concerns of the contemporary world, besides painting frescoes, murals, and doing conservation work on the paintings and classical art of Old Masters. His work has been exhibited in thirty solo and group shows all around Italy. He has recently completed an ambitious project, creating 22 large-size paintings from the *Mahābhārata* that are displayed at the Museum of Sacred Art at Villa Vrindavan. He lives and works in Città di Castello, Perugia, Italy.

Made in the USA
Middletown, DE
16 May 2022

65822377R00035